I0536547

Adirondack Memoir

Camping in the
Moose River Plains
1964-2024

by Matthew T. Beal

Adirondack Memoir

Camping in the Moose River Plains: 1964-2024

Interior design and typesetting by Mark Anderson/Boilerplate Creative

Cover design by Matthew Beal

☂ The Forager Press, LLC

Camillus, NY

www.theforagerpress.com

Printed in the United States of America by The Forager Press

ISBN: 979-8-9992740-1-4

Distributed by Blue Line Book Exchange, Lake Placid NY 12946

www.BlueLineBookExchange.com

Dedication

This book is dedicated to the memory
of both my parents, who introduced me
to the Moose River Plains and taught me
love and respect for the great outdoors,
which I've passed on to family and friends,
as well as the human connection to nature.

It offers benefits of
stress relief, improved mental and
physical health and a sense of
awe and wonder.

I hope this book will encourage others to protect
all the access and boundaries to its beauty.

Matthew T. Beal

Table of Contents

Preface

My name is Matthew Beal and these are my personal campfire memories, stories and adventures from my early childhood and through my adulthood, when I spent my summer vacations and fall and winter trips with my family and friends, camping, hunting and exploring, and observing wildlife and everything the Moose River Plains has to offer, from the beauty of nature's wildlife to the history that was left behind. Over my 58 years, I've watched this forest grow from a young recovering timbered forest mixed with some old forest to the mature forest it is today.

Before I start, here's some history of all its land purchases and original intentions.

Chapter One

The History of the Moose River Plains

The Moose River Recreation Area was once owned primarily by the Gould family's Gould Paper Company, which logged timber from this area. The Gould Paper Company was sold to Georgia-Pacific Corporation in early 1963. Then later that year, on December 14, 1963, Gould Paper Company sold 50,970.11 acres of land to The People of the State of New York for $872,690.08 for public use as a recreational area that is now known as The Moose River Plains Wild Forest. (That's three and a half times the size of Manhattan.)

THIS INDENTURE

Made the *14th* day of December in the year nineteen hundred sixty-three

B e t w e e n GOULD PAPER COMPANY, a corporation organized under the laws of the State of New York, having its principal office at Lyons Falls, New York, party of the first part, and THE PEOPLE OF THE STATE OF NEW YORK, parties of the second part.

W I T N E S S E T H: That the party of the first part, in consideration of EIGHT HUNDRED SEVENTY-TWO THOUSAND SIX HUNDRED NINETY and 08/100 DOLLARS ($872,690.08), lawful money of the United States, paid by the parties of the second part, does hereby grant and release unto the said parties of the second part, and their successors and assigns forever,

ALL THOSE CERTAIN PIECES OR PARCELS OF LAND, situate, lying and being in the Towns of Arietta, Inlet and Morehouse, County of Hamilton, and the Town of Ohio, County of Herkimer, State of New York, being part of Townships 4, Totten and Crossfield's Purchase, and part of Townships 4 and 5, Moose River Tract, more particularly bounded and described as follows:

The Purchase History

The State acquired an original tract of 9,000 acres in the heart of what is now the MRPWF before 1900. In 1948, the Conservation Department issued a permit allowing Gould Paper Company to use an existing wagon road known as the Kenwell Road to haul timber across State lands and to maintain a gate at the end of the road near Limekiln Lake to prevent public access. The Department acquired 15,710 acres surrounding Limekiln Lake from Gould in 1960, then another Gould parcel encompassing Lost Ponds and containing approximately 1,803 acres in 1962. An individual owner sold the State a parcel of 356 acres including Beaver Lake in 1963.

The majority of what is now the MRPWF and the northern part of the West Canada Lake Wilderness was added to the Forest Preserve in 1963, when Gould Paper Company sold the State a tract of 50,970 acres stretching from Horn Lake on the west to Manbury Conservation Mountain on the east. Major subsequent additions included 602 acres surrounding Wakely Dam and the north end of Cedar River Flow from Finch, Pruyn and Company in 1964 and two large parcels acquired from International Paper Company: the 1,120 acre Cellar Mountain parcel in 1986 and a tract of 9,925 acres south of Wakely Mountain in 1988. The larger parcel was acquired subject to an International 987 easement conveyed by IP to Hamilton County for the maintenance of the four miles of Cedar River Road which crossed the parcel.

The New York Department of Conservation

The Department took an active approach to the management of the area then referred to as the Moose River Recreation Area, a name which reflected the intent behind the purchase as told to the People of the state of New York. From the beginning, the Department pursued the development of an extensive road system to provide public access to the remote interior for hunting, trapping, fishing, camping and recreational use. An early Department report indicated that there were about 178 miles of primary gravel roads and an equal extent of secondary and winter roads throughout the former Gould lands. However none of the roads was suitable for public motor vehicle use without significant improvement. Minutes of a meeting of Department staff in December,1963 included an estimated cost of $25,000 for the miles of roads and annual maintenance of 50 bridges.

Starting in 1964, Division of Fish and Wildlife staff used heavy equipment to improve roads initially identified for public use. When the area first was opened to the public on October 23, 1964, the road connecting the Lime-kiln and Cedar River entrances had just been cleared by bulldozer, but remained difficult to traverse. In addition to the LLCR Road, the Rock Dam Road, Otter Brook Road and Sly Pond Loop were open to public use by permit for a total of about 30 miles. Fifty six parking areas were established along the road system. At the entrance gates, cars were assigned parking areas and travel was allowed only to and from those areas. The public could use four wheel drive vehicles or tire chains. Pickups with slip on campers were permitted from the start, but because the roads were not yet suitable, trailers were not permitted.

In a road plan adopted in 1965, roads to be designated were divided into three categories. Twenty two miles would be first priority roads, open to all traffic; 30.5 miles would be second priority roads, open only to four wheel drive vehicles; and 7.5 miles would be administrative roads restricted to use by Department staff for crossing private property.

In the first years after the area was opened to the public, access remained difficult because of the effects of weather on road conditions. In the summer of 1965, work needed to make the roads passable delayed opening until July 1. In order to minimize fire danger and facilitate the disposal of trash, the public was allowed to camp only in areas adjacent to the roads and for a maximum of three days. Trash receptacles eventually were provided at most campsites, and Department staff collected trash twice a week through the 1970s. The trash was deposited at a dump site south of the LLCR Road east of Helldiver Pond right next to site #56 and across from #57. Today there is a state cabin on the off road to the old inner transfer dump just off the main road.

The road crew worked steadily year by year to improve the roads with the intention of ultimately allowing them to be traveled safely by cars. After the extensive logging by Gould, especially after the 1950 Blowdown, much of the area was occupied by thick, low vegetation, and the tops of harvested and wind thrown trees. Foot travel was difficult. To allow hunters to more easily travel through more remote areas in search of game, Fish and Wildlife staff used a bulldozer to clear and extend logging roads and skid trails to serve as foot trails, starting in the late 1960s.

Trails cleared in this way include routes to Mitchell Ponds, Bear Pond, Lost

Ponds, Cellar Pond, Beaver Lake, Sly Pond and Squaw Lake, as well as those along Benedict Creek and Butter Brook. A number of routes cleared at that time are now within the West Canada Lake Wilderness, including the trails to Balsam, Stink and Horn Lake and Falls Pond. Many of the cleared routes extended beyond the trails currently marked and maintained. A map prepared by Jack Harnish, a member of the crew that did the trail clearing work, is on file with the Department.

The minutes of the December 9, 1963 Department staff meeting mentioned above included in the list of recommendations for the operation of the area that the Department should establish several small camping areas to include tables, fireplaces and latrines throughout the area adjacent to the roads where parties could park and camp. By 1965 the Department began constructing campsites and installing fireplaces, picnic tables and privies, which were built in a field just west of the Cedar River entrance.

At each suitable location along the road system, a bulldozer was used to make a short access driveway and level an area where a car or pickup truck could park and camp. A number of campsites were created at former log landings. Many of the areas originally intended as roadside parking areas later were converted to campsites. Campsite construction was completed by the late 1960s.

Because of the importance of the Plains as a deer wintering area, the Department's game management staff began studying the area in 1931. Hunting and fishing advocates such as the Adirondack Conservation Council supported the acquisition of the Plains and the development of its roads, trails and campsites for hunting and fishing access. In 1965 and 1966, with federal Pittman Robertson Act funding, 30 log landings were graded for hunter parking access and 30,000 trees were planted in the Plains area as an experiment intended to provide winter deer shelter.

In 1965 housing was constructed for the Limekiln and Cedar River gatekeepers. The possibility of a use fee was discussed, but no fee was charged during the early years. During the 1976 season, the Department charged a fee of $1.50 or $2.00 per car. A subsequent assessment determined that most of the revenue generated by the fee was offset by the costs of staffing and administration. The fee was discontinued the following year.

Work to clear hunter access trails by bulldozer continued for a few years. However, after repeated incidents of public motor vehicle travel on these trails, 16 barriers were installed in 1970, and motor vehicles no longer were used to maintain the trails. Also in 1970, the original road plan was changed to close 22.5 miles of the original.

Management and Policy

Moose River Plains Wild Forest Revised Draft Unit Management Plan/Draft Generic Environmental Impact Statement   July 2010

30.5 miles of secondary roads were opened to the public and retained as administrative roads. The other eight miles, consisting of the beginning of the Otter Brook truck trail and the road to the Indian River, were upgraded to primary roads, and the gate at the Otter Brook Bridge was removed.

As work progressed over the years and the condition of the road system improved, the Department relaxed restrictions on the types of vehicles the public could drive. In the late 1960s the Department decided to allow motorhomes up to 22 feet long to travel the roads through big game hunting season, as long as they had tire chains. It was thought that they were less likely to get stuck than vehicles towing camping trailers, which the Department continued to prohibit. However, pressure to allow trailers began early and continued to grow. After Department staff conducted an assessment of the roads and determined that they had been sufficiently improved, they decided to allow trailers beginning around 1980.

For several years after the Department first erected wood signs in the MRPWF, they were repeatedly damaged by black bears. To prevent further destruction, metal signs were installed in 1975. Most are still there today.

A detailed Department map prepared in 1977 shows 222 campsite and parking area locations along the road system. The map provides an inventory of the structures at each site, showing the prevalence of fireplaces, picnic tables and privies at the time. Twenty sites were closed in 1980 after the reclassification of the southwestern portion of the area to wilderness, when the road to the Indian River was gated at Indian Lake. The campsites were not given numbers on the ground until the 1980s. A number of original sites that had fallen into disuse were bypassed when the numbers were assigned, so that in 2008 there were 170 numbered sites. In 2006 sites 7, 34, 66, 73, 90, 119a, 130, and site 1 at Cedar River Flow were modified and designated as accessible sites.

In recent years, maintenance activities have focused on keeping the road system in passable condition, replacing inadequate culverts and doing trail maintenance.

In 2001, four gravel pits were reclaimed and replanted. In 1996, an engineering evaluation was completed for the public motor vehicle roads in the unit. The report focused on eight major and twelve minor culvert problem areas and made recommendations for replacing existing culverts with new structures of sufficient capacity to handle a design storm of 100 year occurrence probability with a snowmelt allowance. Between 2000 and 2005, 11 of the 12 minor sites, with the exception of site 10B, were addressed, and site 5A of the major sites was the only one complete.

When the Moose River Recreation Area was first opened to the public, use levels were relatively high. During the big game hunting season in 1964, 2,021 vehicles with 5,764 passengers signed in. Though the area originally was purchased and developed for use by hunters, trappers and anglers, the first 10 day report filed after the 1965 opening on July 1 indicated that 75 percent of visitors were campers and sight seers. In 1966, 7,809 people signed in as anglers and 23,408 camper days were recorded during big game hunting season, about 6,000 of which were recorded for campsites beyond the Otter Brook Bridge. Big game hunters were very successful in the early years, harvesting 373 deer and 15 bears in 1966 and a high of 404 deer in 1968. Deer harvest levels declined sharply after 1969, with 77 harvested in 1970 and 11 in 1971.

Since the 1970s, the number of deer taken by hunters has increased, and in recent years harvest numbers have nearly returned to the levels recorded in the 1960s. The MRPWF remains popular with hunters, trappers and anglers.

Early management included the adoption of a number of regulations in 1972. These regulations, which still apply to public use of the area, require visitors to register at the Cedar River and Limekiln entrances, require the use of tire chains after October 1 except on 4 wheel drive vehicles, prohibit snowmobile operation during the big game hunting season, and prohibit the use of motorcycles and motorized bicycles.

Current conditions may warrant the elimination of the registration requirement and the prohibition against motorcycle use. The Moose River Plains Wild forest today is approximately 84,000 acres.

For historical information on the early logging days in the Moose River Plains get Life Around the Indian Clearing and other books written by my dear friend, William J. O'Hern.

Chapter Two

The Golden Years

1960s-1970s

Let's begin my family and friends camping memories and stories in late Fall, 1964, at theCedar River flow gate entrance into the Moose River Plains Recreation Area. It was the first day of the official opening for public access. My father had heard of this newly acquired piece of public land called the Moose River Plains Recreation Area and decided to do a hunting trip with a few friends. Below are some photos of what it looked like

The Moose River Plains opened for the public - 1964

from old logging roads and a few campsites.

A recreational area is any place designed or used for leisure and relaxation. This includes bodies of water like lakes, ponds, rivers, and streams when they're open to the public. Areas commonly used for activities such as hunting, fishing, bird watching, wildlife observation, exploring, bike riding, hiking, or camping are also considered recreational areas.

The main corridor heading east coming in from Inlet side
looking towards Bradley Mountain - 1964

This photo was taken from site #35 in 1964. It's the Sly Pond Road log bridge crossing the Moose River. I believe there were a total of 18+ of these log type bridges throughout the Moose River Plains. Only one exists today. It's on the trail to Lost Ponds.

Two of my dad's hunting buddies standing on the Sly Pond road bridge looking towards site #35. The truck is parked in the campsite.

Lost the exhaust system in 1965, as some of the 4WD off-roads were rough, mostly single-lane deep ruts with grass in the middle except the main corridor roads.

One of the most desired campsites, because it's on water, the South Branch of the Moose River, site #87. A lot of that site has washed away since, but is still being used today.

Site #87, looking to the left at site #86. It's still there, just not used much.

To my dad and his friends, it was nature's wildlife paradise—"God's Country"—and from that trip, Dad made plans to bring our family—our mom, me and my brother—camping and introduce us to the beauty in the wilderness and the great outdoors. It was a true Recreation Area in a primitive setting with a wide range of all types of views, all of which were outstanding. There was the understanding that this area was going to be well maintained and managed for future generations to have access to it as it is, and all its beauty that lay within.

In 1965-1966 I was at Red River site #79 with my family. A log bridge was once here. It was washed out in the mid '80s and replaced with a culvert pipe which exists today.

My brother Arty and our mom, mid 60s, at Red River site #79.

This photo was taken from the Log Bridge on the Red River in 1966 looking at Site #79, where we set up our camp.

Photo, site #79 at Red River with the old log bridge in the background.

Photo of me at 11+ months old. I celebrated my first birthday
in the Plains at the last campsite on the Indian River.

This photo shows the farthest point from either of the gates and is the end campsite on the Indian River Road, about 20 feet in the woods off the road's loop dead end turn-around and the trailhead to Balsam, Stink and Horn lakes, access to the West Canada Wilderness.

Photo below shows me hiking on my dad's back, not that I remember much from that age, but it surely drove me to love nature and the great outdoors.

The Balsam, Stink, and Horn Lake Trail

This was a beautiful, mostly flat hike through a healthy balsam forest, and the smell of those balsams was so strong and fresh. With just a little breeze, If I close my eyes I can still smell those balsams and the crisp Adirondack air with the view of Stink Mountain in the distance, we'd drive to the end and hike a few miles to Balsam, Stink and Horn lakes and Ice Cave trail every year. What great access point it was into the West Canada Wilderness Area.After the hike, we'd return to Indian River Road and walk along it, exploring the various old logging roads branching off, some of which were situated behind campsites. Walking allowed us to observe more details than driving; for instance, I remeYearsmber seeing a small unnamed pond with floating logs that were used during the logging era for trucks and tractors to cross when the ponds froze in winter. Behind another campsite, we discovered the "Big Eddy," a large area of water flowing in the opposite direction of the main current due to an obstruction in the river.

This was the road/trail just as you crossed the Indian River
log bridge heading to Balsam Lake, 1968.

Me and my dad in the early 70s on the Balsam Lake/log road trail.
I'm holding a stick, a piece of nature in my hand, as always.

My brother Arty and I are parked at the end of Indian River Road.
We were learning how to drive.

As I grew older, we occasionally camped at several of these primitive sites, staying for one to three nights. These campsites lacked outhouses. Some featured state-made concrete or stone fireplaces with grates, while others had simple arrangements of rocks and cinder blocks to contain campfires. All of them were equipped with picnic tables, most located on or near the Indian River. Every few years, we revisited this area to check on the campsites, and our father taught us how to drive on this road as we matured.

I did camp a few nights there with my dad in 1980, prior to its closure a the end of the season when the Moose River Plains Recreation Area border was moved and that area was added to West Canada Wilderness, pushing the Moose River Plains boundary back to Little Indian Lake, Site #149. A barrier was installed, closing miles of roads and access to all the campsites on it. I still hike the Indian River Road and the area every few years with my kids, and I have watched how fast it has completely overgrown.

The road/trail isn't even accessible for any fire control if ever needed. It's not at all maintained, nor is the area managed, as it has become almost erased as a place for people to visit. I navigate by recalling the landmarks around me. It is a significant loss for future generations, and those who have discovered and cherished the Moose River Plains Wild Forest over the last 25 years are unable to access other areas they could explore.

Only through collective advocacy can we restore access to these areas, allowing camping and preventing the closure of existing roads and campsites.

While I support protecting the forest and maintaining its pristine condition, it must be accessible and managed properly to ensure a healthy forest that supports wildlife habitats. (There are some photos from this area, past and present, in Chapter 7.)

Below is a NYSDEC Report from Department records regarding its activity.

The first 10 day report filed after the 1965 opening on July 1 indicated that 75 % of visitors were campers and sight seers. In 1966, 7,809 people signed in as anglers and 23,408 camper days were recorded during big game hunting season.

VERY IMPORTANT Note : ...about 6,000 of which were recorded for campsites beyond the Otter Brook bridge, noted as the most beautiful area and with the most campsites on water.

Big game hunters were very successful in the early years, harvesting 373 deer and 15 bears in 1966 and a high of 404 deer in 1968. Deer harvest levels declined sharply after 1969, with 77 harvested in 1970 and 11 in 1971. Since the 1970s the number of deer taken by hunters has decreased.

I met up with Gary Lee (retired ranger), who managed the Moose River Plains for over 30 years, to review my history in this book for accuracy, and said that he was the one who wrote this report for the NYSDEC.Only one log was left at the Indian River crossing Trailhead in the West Canada Wilderness to the Balsam, Stink and Horn lake trails. Crossing that river was no fun for a little kid when that river was high and raging. That was me, YES!!

My brother Arty and me and my dad, 1971.

The sign in the photo below was just as you got to Balsam Lake, about half a mile from the Indian River Bridge. This was the old wooden trail marker off the road. Most of these signs were replaced in the mid 70s by metal ones because the bears were chewing on the wooden ones.

From Balsam, we'd hike to Stink Lake and then Horn Lake. At that time, no fishing was allowed at Horn Lake. It was used as a natural fish hatchery. From Horn, there was an old wagon/log trail, the Ice Cave Mountain Trail.

The South of Balsam Lake

Chapter Three

Camping and Exploring in the MRP Recreation Area

1970s-80s

Photos of the second-generation map and camping regulations from the 1970s up to 1980 show the original boundary of the Moose River Plains Recreation Area. (The first generation was the same, only in a different font.)

MOOSE RIVER
Recreation Area

N. Y. S. DEPARTMENT OF ENVIRONMENTAL CONSERVATION
DIVISION OF LANDS AND FORESTS, ALBANY, N. Y. 12233

Situated in the western part of Hamilton County, the Moose River Recreation Area is sometimes known as the Gould Tract, having been purchased from the Gould Paper Company in December, 1963. Approximately 50,000 acres in size, it is surrounded by State lands of older vintage, making a sizeable area for the hunter, fisherman and sportsman.

The Region was lumbered by the Gould Paper Company with the last cutting taking place just prior to the State of New York taking title. A maze of abandoned logging roads exists throughout the area as a result of these logging operations.

Terrain varies from the flatness of the Moose River Plains to the gentle and often steep pitches of the adjoining ridges and mountains.

It is a remote region with much to offer the individual or group who enjoy wilderness camping, fishing or hunting.

Drainage throughout is generally westerly or southwesterly with most ponds and streams eventually emptying into the south branch of the Moose River.

Entrance to the area may be gained from the east or the west. At the west end of the area the main entrance is at Limekiln Lake and is reached by a road running south from Route 28 a short distance east of the village of Inlet. The entrance from the east is at Cedar River Flow (Wakely) and is reached by proceeding west from Indian Lake Village on Route 28, turning left on the Cedar River Road (a town highway)

Front cover of the Moose River Recreation Area pamphlet.

Adirondack Memoir 25

and following it to its terminus.

Facilities provided are primitive in keeping with the general atmosphere of the region. Access roads which traverse the area are narrow with many steep pitches. They are considered as unimproved and may be impassable following even a light snow fall.

Travel is restricted to passenger cars and trucks up to and including 1 ton capacity. During the hunting season all vehicles entering the area, unless they are four-wheel drive, will be required to have tire chains that fit the vehicle. No trailers will be permitted beyond either gate. No motorcycles or motorized bicycles are permitted.

All persons entering the area must register with the Caretaker at the gate. The Department of Environmental Conservation may close either or both gates to entry by vehicles at any time it is felt that traveling conditions are hazardous or the capacity of the camping and parking area is reached.

Hunting Regulations

1. No person shall discharge a firearm in a parking or camping area or on or across a road now open for vehicular travel.

2. No road hunting will be permitted.

3. Upon leaving the area, each permittee shall complete the game take information and allow examination of game taken.

Fishing Regulations

1. Car top boats and canoes are permitted. No outboard motors shall be allowed in the area.

2. The use of fish as bait, either dead or alive, is not permitted within the area.

3. Upon leaving the area, each permittee shall complete and return to the Caretaker the fishing report card.

4. Fishing is not permitted in Horn Lake.

Camping Regulations

1. All persons must register with caretaker in charge.

2. Tent camping will be allowed only on camping sites as assigned by the Caretaker. A camping permit will be required for periods exceeding three nights. No trailers of any kind will be allowed.

3. Parking for day use will be in parking lots provided for this purpose.

Within this recreation area, there are two parcels of private lands as outlined on the map. From the Cedar River Gate access is provided by

Interior page of the Moose River Plains Recreation Area pamphlet.

26   Adirondack Memoir

Guidelines for Hikers and Campers

Our forest and mountain environment offers opportunities for recreational pleasure, appreciation of nature, and a rejuvenating escape from the urban world. Help care for our wilderness environment and enhance the enjoyment of it for yourself and those that follow by observing these simple guidelines.

- What you carry in, carry out. Leave the woods cleaner than you found them. Bring a refuse bag and carry out more than you carried in.
- Observe and enjoy wildlife and plant life but leave them undisturbed.
- Observe all posted regulations and be considerate of fellow hikers and campers.

For Your Safety

- Plan your trip carefully according to routes and time available. Carry the latest guidebooks and maps.
- Always let someone know where you are going and when you expect to return.
- Check weather reports before you set out.
- Be prepared for unexpected emergencies. Carry a compass, pocket knife, waterproof matches, high energy food items such as candy, a first aid kit and extra protective clothing.
- In case of accident, at least one person should remain with the injured person. Others should carefully note the location and contact the local forest ranger.
- Notify the local forest ranger if any of your companions become lost.
- If you become lost, keep calm, stay where you are and keep warm. If you feel you can try and find your way out, remember that following streams downhill will nearly always lead you back to signs of habitation.

Department of Environmental Conservation
Region 5 Offices

Regional Headquarters
Ray Brook, N. Y. 12977
518-891-1370

Regional Office
P. O. Box 220
Hudson Street Extension
Warrensburg, N. Y. 12885
518-623-3671

Regional Office
Northville, N. Y. 12134
518-925-2660

LF-P22 (10M 2/76)

Back page of the Moose River Plains Recreation Area pamphlet.

Adirondack Memoir 27

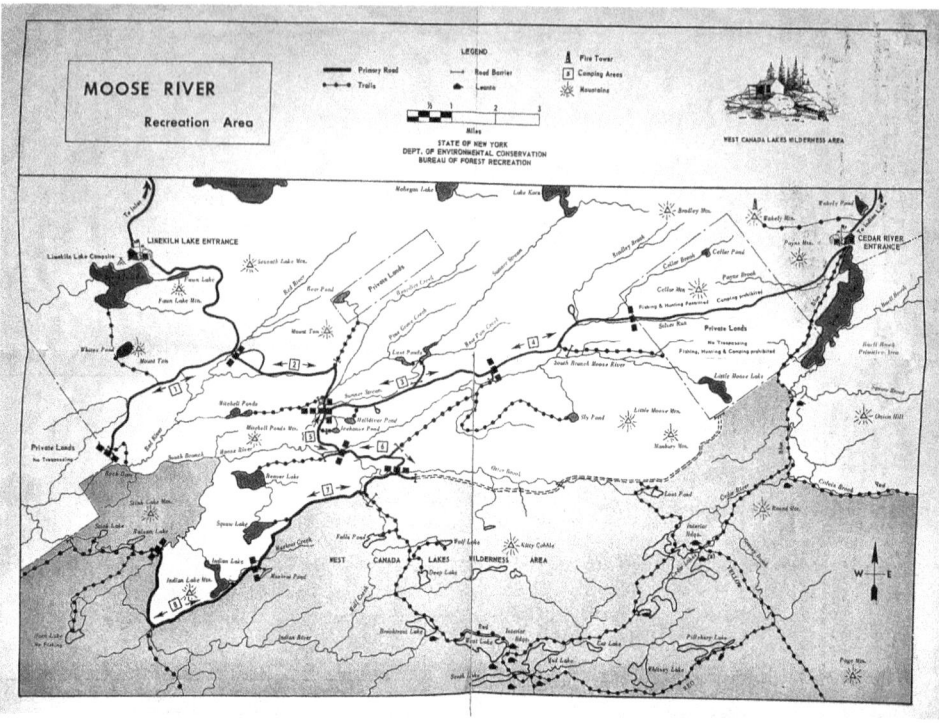

Photo of the Moose River Plains map showing its original borders
and access roads at the time (fold-out of the previous pages).

The Indian River and the surrounding area were very popular for big game and for fishing native brookies. I'd always see someone fishing there. I'd see more wildlife and game in this area as well. During this time, fish were having a hard time surviving due to their recovery from the acid rain. Back then a few lakes were acid dead. Brooktrout Lake was one of them, and it has slowly been able to naturally recover to sustain fish life.

The state had Gary Lee, who worked as a ranger during the golden years of managing the entire area, improving the roads, supervising, and managing the trails. The state had a crew working all summer on a new parking area with two entrances and two culvert pipes, providing another access point into the West Canada Wilderness area trailhead to Balsam, Stink, and Horn Lakes.

Later that year, they closed off the Indian River Road and reclassified the Indian River as a wild river, closing all the primitive campsites and the road. The borderlines of the Moose River Plains were pushed back to Lit-

28   Adirondack Memoir

tle Indian Lake. This was followed by closures of roads and access points, which marked the beginning of reduced management of the Moose River Plains by the State of New York. The Moose River Plains could have been grandfathered in after its purchase in 1963 to remain as a recreational

Photo from 1970 of me and my brother Arty in an old wooden boat at Little Indian Lake that has been there since the 1950s, from what I was told by sources.

area, with its primitive wilderness for outdoorsmen.

The following are photos from 1970 early summer camping at Lost Ponds, Sites #48 and #49 with one of our neighbors. We did mostly fishing and

The lower campsite #49 at Lost Ponds, surrounded by pines in a breathing forest.

The same lower campsite at Lost Ponds, as of 2024.
There are fewer pines and it's a bit choked up.

1970: Upper campsite #48 at Lost Ponds.

1971, camping at Otter Brook site #118. This was a riverside campsite.
The river & fireplace is to the left.

canoeing at Lost Ponds and watched the bears come to our site every night.

In 1971, we set up camp at Otter Brook. The concrete bridge had just been completed at that time. The original log road passed through the campsite to the other side. The Otter Brook Truck Trail/Indian Lake Road, along with the old wire barrier, is still present in the forest and well overgrown. This area contained numerous old logging buildings and many off-road wagon trails suitable for hiking.

One notable trail is the Otter Brook Truck Trail, which heads east from the "T" junction as you cross the Otter Brook Bridge, following Otter Brook around Little Moose Mountain all the way to Little Moose Lake. This trail has now become a bushwhack trail intended for advanced hikers.

Photo from the campsite looking across Otter Brook you can see where the old log road once crossed the river then a log bridge was installed about 100 ft to the East and later was replaced with a concrete bridge

Otter Brook Bridge camping trip in 1971 with our friends, the Seitzes. We're having a great time swimming in Otter Brook near the newly-completed concrete bridge.

Throughout my life, I have traversed almost every old truck trail in the Moose River Plains.

The next photo was taken in 1971 near site #76, looking from the road overlooking the Red Plains (near the Red River). The deer would herd in

The Red Plains (Red River Area) from the road.

this area, which is why it is called "Moose River Plains." The berm visible here was once an old logging road, now the Mitchell Pond Loop trail. To the far right was site #76A. Gary Lee (Ranger at the time) told me it was closed for one or two years to protect a Golden Eagle nesting in the area. This region had abundant wild berries and blueberries that we used in pancakes. They also served as a food source for wildlife. Gary Lee mentioned that controlled burns were conducted in this area to reduce wildfire risks, improve wildlife habitats, and restore natural ecosystems.

We would pick different campsites each time we'd go camping because each area had something different to offer, from old logging history to the wildlife and the various types of trees in the forest and meadows. We saw

1972. We'd just arrived at site #24, Silver Run. We were still setting up camp. You can still see the old Butter Brook log road/trail across the river and just make out Little Moose Mountain in the far left distance from this site. At the time, the views were amazing. That lasted up until the late 80s, but the area has rapidly become overgrown and the State started reducing it's full time staff.

Our camp set up at site #24, Silver Run.

The Seitz family

beaver ponds, mountain views, rivers and lakes. We would fish and canoe them and hike all the trails, as they all were well managed and maintained.

We made a rock wall on the river's edge to keep our drinks cool in the water, but overnight the water rose so high that some of our drinks got

Ten out of fourteen rainy days in a row never kept us from enjoying everything about being in the wilderness, exploring and checking out all the other campsites. It's only water.

Photo at Silver Run below shows how high the water was after ten days of rain.
A conservation officer came to the rescue and got what was left of our drinks.

My brother Arty and me. Silver Run was raging

washed away. The river was up to the fireplace, and the conservation officer went into the river holding a rope to get what was left of our sodas and drinks for us. There was an old log road that crossed Silver Run, located opposite campsite #24. At that time, there was only a cable barrier, which we used as a towel line, and a 55-gallon garbage can for our trash. This garbage was collected daily by a New York State conservation worker. Later, an iron gate was installed, which remains to this day. The "You carry it in, You carry it out" rule was implemented in the 1980s. It's a good rule.

Me inside one of the buildings, half collapsed and not yet burned by the State.
Of course I'm holding a leaf, a piece of nature's treasure in my hand.
I was so amazed at the structure and the history behind it.

1972. Old log camp across Silver Run.

We explored the log road across Silver Run to an old logging building about ¼ of a mile in. The old road went to the Moose River. This was a piece of logging history.

There's a lot of history left behind, like old 55-gallon drums, skid tractors,

1973. Photo above is my brother and me site #101.

old cars, and other items left by previous land owners and loggers. There are a few of these relics over by Bradley Brook, Site #14-#18. It was an old log road and there are still a few cars back in there off the old logging road.

You just couldn't keep me from being one with everything about nature. I took it all in and loved everything: the touch of the water, the sand and the rocks. We hiked all the trails and fished and canoed all the lakes and ponds in the Moose River Plains.

We'd just arrived at 7AM at site #101 after driving five hours from Long Island, where I grew up. I'd always jump out of the truck as soon as we arrived and kiss the ground where we would camp for the next 12+ days with our family and our friends, the Seitzes. I'd take a deep breath and fill my lungs with that crisp, fresh Adirondack air. There is nothing like it.

Our campfires went basically 24/7. We'd often just sit in silence for a while, listening to everything nature was singing, from the crackling of the pine in the fire to the wind in the distance to a night owl hooting or a coyote howling at the moon. Nature's music, and the bright stars above were beautiful and soothing to my mind and soul.

This campsite had some big pine trees. We would climb them, then call out to our parents, "Hey, come over here!"

40   Adirondack Memoir

"Where are you?" they'd call back.

"We're up here, look up!" we'd reply.

Then our parents, with their hearts in their throats, would shout, "GET DOWN NOW!"

That's me up in the top of the pine tree. Can you see me now?

I don't think we'll run out of wood for a while.

With the raccoon checking out our camp, set up in his home area, there was always something to entertain us.

Bears were regulars every night in the late 70s through the late 80s as our night entertainment. We'd know when they were around because our dogs' teeth would start to chatter and the hair on their backs would stand straight up. We'd know it was time to put the dogs in the truck. Ten minutes later, we would hear the bears in the woods and smell their sour scent ! Yes, that's how close they were. All of our flashlights were on, shining into the woods until we saw their green glowing eyes. Then we would just make noise and bang pots and pans to send them on their way back into the woods until the next night, when they would be back. One night we were sitting by the fire and turned around to look at the picnic table and a bear was on the table eating cookies we forgot to put away! Oops! We would put the clothes we were wearing from the day in a plastic bag and in the car with our food and coolers, never leaving anything out and especially never bringing food into our tent. Lesson 101, ha-ha! We would put moth balls around our tents and campsites to hide any scent of food.

Every day one of the conservation workers would come by to talk and give us any information about the area and the wildlife that happened to be around, maybe something we'd missed and could go explore. They set up a bear trap at site #100, about 1,000 feet away, and caught a bear, but guess what? We had a bear that night again.

I think there were three to five full-time workers in the Plains. They would use the soil/sand from the sand pits to do road repairs, using the soil from within to replenish itself. The sandpit over by Red River was also where they would make new fireplaces for campsites that needed it. They would bring all of the broken fireplaces and grills there and reuse the grills that were good. The grills back then were three times as thick as the thin bars they use today. We called that area "the fireplace graveyard."

Lillian was one of the last full-time workers. Up until about the 1990s, they were always doing something—trail maintenance, filling washouts, removal of trees across the trail, cutting with a cutting bar, managing the vegetation growth on the trails for fire control (as agreed in the original purchase contract regarding fire prevention), search and rescue if ever needed, and caring for campsites and the roads. All of this was well managed by Forest Ranger Gary Lee and his work crew, We would see him and speak to him often.

I think having New York State conservation officers in the Plains helped ensure the proper use and respect of the lands. People left their campsites clean, without bottle caps, wrappers, or small trash. There were also no cut live trees around the campsites. After all, live trees do not burn.

The rock is still there, but the surroundings have completely changed. I am very observant of the terrain. There is something defiant in the terrain. It won't change, only the surroundings will change naturally as the forest grows in.

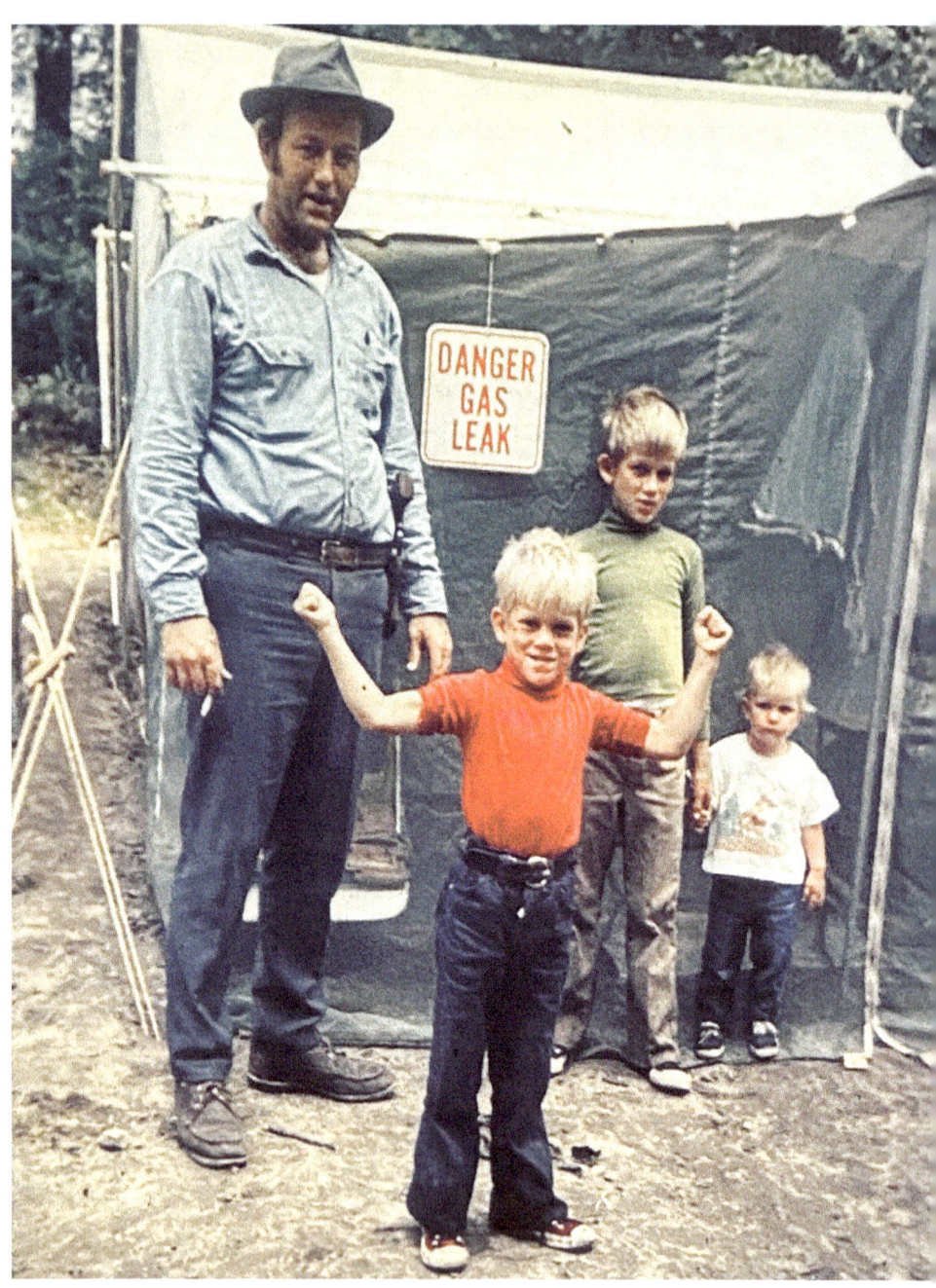

I'm with my Dad, my brother Arty and Dee Seitz.
My expression says I'm so happy to be there and ready for the day's adventure.
(Gotta love the 'gas leak' sign. Franks 'n' Beans, our family humor classic.)

44   Adirondack Memoir

Photo taken looking up towards campsite #101, hiking a short trail to Otter Brook.
Then it was just high vegetation, but in 2024 it's a full-grown forest.

The same trail, looking down from campsite #101.
Notice the big rock on the trail, and on the left it slopes down to Otter Brook.

1974-1975 found us camping at Lost Ponds, Sites #48 and #49 with our friends the Seitz's for another 14 days. Site #49 had a black pipe water spring. It's all grown in now, but the pipe is still there. If you look for it, you'll find it.

Me after fourteen days, when it was time to go home.

Some late fall camping, 1974. After another 7-10 days, our truck was packed to go home and I stayed under the truck because I wanted to stay longer. I think my dad gave up after about an hour, and my cousin was able to convince me to come out by saying, "We'll come right back as soon as we get home."

Watching bears (from a distance) was a regular wildlife entertainment. Along with the moth balls around our tent and site, we used common-sense bear awareness rules. One time we went on a hike and forgot to put our metal Coleman cooler, which had a center latch,away in the car. We came back to the cooler's corner ends bent up and all the food and dry ice eaten.

Site #49, shows the 'Spring' sign at the campsite and another bear in the daytime.

Back at our campsite, we always kept ourselves busy building free-standing timber forts, rafts, climbing trees and swimming in Sumner Stream.

For our 24/7 campfire, we'd buy a truckload of slab wood from Levi Lumber in Inlet. In the next two photos, you can see the fort my brother and I built in the background. We used downed pine from the woods and rope.

Hiking to Mitchell Pond for a day of canoeing and fishing.
It was another beautiful pond with good fishing.
If you look northeast, you'll see Mount Tom.

50   Adirondack Memoir

Mitchell Pond, 1973

Raft we built at Sumner Stream, Mitchell Pond, 1973

Adirondack Memoir 51

1974, A pioneering tower we built at Lost Ponds campsite.

The pond is about one mile from the barrier, with an old log bridge crossing Sumner Stream. The trail splits: left, to the pond site, right, around the back side of the pond. There are old log roads, mostly overgrown and hard to follow, but identifiable by tree line growth and personal landmarks like big rocks.

I was told by my neighbor, who worked for Gould Paper as a logger and a forest manager from the 40s until 1963, that some of the largest pines were harvested there. They practiced selective cutting, where trees too large to hug were left standing. During summer, no logging occurred, and stewards replanted trees and managed wildlife, including controlled burns. Some cut logs remain near the trail as you approach Lost Ponds.

The pond was a hot spot for brook trout in the late 70s-90s and remains popular. It's a beautiful setting, with solid rock creating a natural echo effect. Near the log bridge on Sumner Stream, there are remnants of an old water lock and dam used to float logs downstream.

52   Adirondack Memoir

Lost Ponds

Old water log locks on Sumner Stream and our pup, Noah.

Two photos way down Sumner Stream. just past the old water lock. Depending on the spring rain water levels you can walk the high grass banks along it.

Sumner Stream

54   Adirondack Memoir

1975. One memory during that trip that I'll never forget is the day we went on a hike to Rock Dam. We did some swimming and I got a leech on my toe. It sucked on my toe real good, and my dad cut it off with his pocket knife. I still have the scar.

We would walk the main road for miles and down all the old log roads, watching all the wildlife, bald eagles, and hawks, and tracking deer, rabbits, turtles, bobcats, fishers, etc. The forest was a more open, healthy, breathing forest then and wildlife had more free movement. We occasionally saw coyotes in the borrow sand pit.

My personal thoughts are to never disturb or disrupt the wildlife. This is their environment and their home. Just observe them, for we are just their guests. This is what I teach my kids.

We walked almost every old log road. Some went nowhere and some went to old cars, trucks and logging equipment from the 1930-50s. There were many logging camps all over, some still standing until the mid '70s and not yet burned by the State. Old log sleds left in the woods off Sites #53-55, and a concrete slab are all that remains of one logging camp. It looks like it's where they did repairs on the logging equipment.

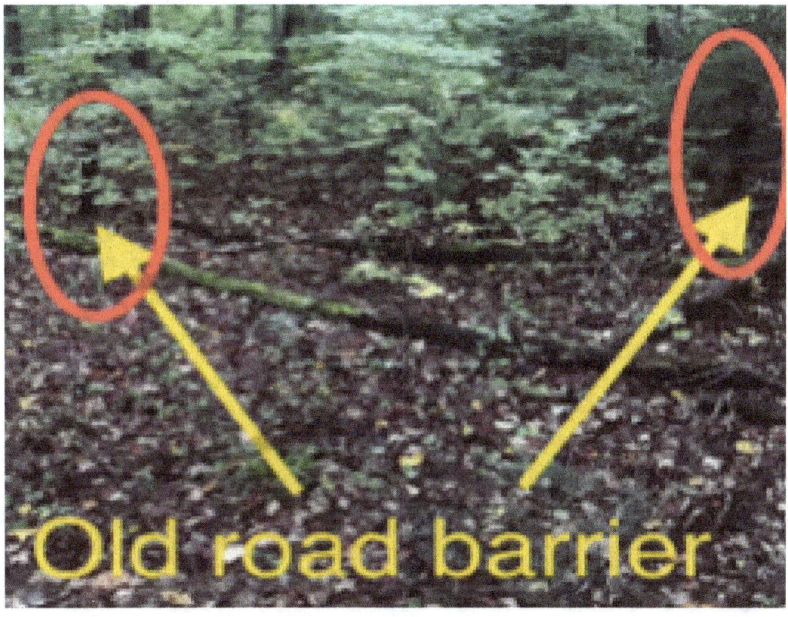

The old log road across from Otter Brook Site #118. The old wire barrier posts are still there in the woods. You could follow some of these old roads by the older growth trees on the sides and the younger growth in the middle.

1976. Little Indian Lake and waking up to 6"-8" of snow
and our canvas army tent canopy collapsed. Fun.

1976 hunting trip. Even with the snow, it was a successful one with a ten-point buck
from the Indian River area. We'd drive to the end of Indian River Road and
cross the Indian River to hunt. This area was great for big buck hunting.

In 1978, I was a guide for a Boy Scout group 192 from Bellmore Long Island, introducing them to the wilderness and I took them on the trail to Balsam Lake, explaining what types of wildlife lives in the area and what types of trees were around us, as well as what berries they could and couldn't eat along the way, and how to use a map and compass.

Indian River crossing at the end of the Indian River Road and the Moose River Plains boundary line, and where the West Canada Wilderness began.

Crossing the Indian River and showing them the remains of an old log bridge.

On the log road/trail to Balsam, Stink and Horn lakes and the West Canada Wilderness.
Photo is about 1.5 miles from the Indian River.
The trail today is unrecognizable as it is a full grown forest

1978. Boy Scout Troop 192 camping at Lost Ponds. Doing their morning salute and ceremony.

Chapter Four

Reclassification In MRP

The Start Of Access to Land/Road/Campsite and River Closures and Camping Memories

1980s-1990s

1980 brought changes to the Moose River Plains when the Indian River was classified as a wild river and the Moose River Plains boundaries were moved to the far end of Little Indian Lake and added to the West Canada Wilderness Area, closing miles of the Indian River Road and all the primitive campsites along it.

We set up camp that last year down Indian River Road. The site we took, #152, was just off the Indian River at the tail end of Camping Area 8, a primitive camping area. At that time in the Moose River Plains, the State had done away with site numbers. None of the ones in this area ever had numbers, but for a while the numbered sites had signs reading "Camping areas 1 through 8." There was no specific number of sites in each area. Once numbers were put back, if you counted from site #149 at Little Indian Lake, our site would have been #152 was on the Indian River

This is the last camping area #7 to #8 sign which was the deepest, most remote section of the Moose River Plains along the Indian River. It was very primitive camping, and a good access point to another entry into the 168,920 acre West Canada Wilderness Area.

Old Camping Area sign #7 to #8

The Swamp Rat Hunting Crew, 1980

In the 1980s, we took a four-day hunting trip at Lost Ponds. We had sites #48, #49, and #45, a walk-in site with our outfitters tent with a small military M1941 pot belly wood stove. The site was just past the trail barrier, about 100 feet on the right, where once was a logging building, now long gone except for the old stove that kept the loggers warm, which is still in the woods on the edge of the swamp.

Site #4, closed many years now.

Site #45, on the Lost Ponds trail, with me splitting some wood.

Site #45

We'd always make sure to leave a campsite cleaner than when we got it with some firewood for the next person, but rarely did we get a dirty site until after the late '90's-2000s, when there were no more State employees working in the Plains managing the area and keeping a few bad camping apples in line.

For me, it was more of another fantastic camping trip. I just loved being out in the woods.

I'd get up just before dawn to prep for Moose River Homefries. I'd start them cooking on an open cherrywood fire in a huge frying pan for eight. I'd always get cherry firewood for cooking anything on the grill or frying pan. It gives your food a sweet smoked flavor. Pine is good for a crackling and smoke-smelling fire; it's a soft wood so it burns quickly. A good hardwood fire is hotter and lasts longer and no embers.

Moose River Homefries

I'd walk a few miles and do a little bushwhacking off a trail and just sit for hours in the woods, taking it all in, the morning smell, the fresh, cool air, the dew on the leaves and the sun shining through the trees, a few birds singing. It was pure peace.

My friend Rob and I hiked this old log road to Sly Pond (Sly Pond Road). This pond is noted for its elevation. There are no fish in the pond. The trail never was one I'd recommend. It's mostly like a riverbed and it's wet. The log bridge was removed around 1984, and that was the end of that trail. The Moose River at that location is deep. The trail now is off Otter Brook Road, where an old road ties into the old Sly Pond Road. It is still rough, and it's a longer trail now.

1984 was the last year this bridge was there. It was either dynamited by the State or the river reached its peak and washed it away.

64   Adirondack Memoir

1985 camping at Otter Brook

In 1985, I was at Otter Brook river site #118 with some friends I took for a weekend of primitive camping. The State concrete fireplace at the time was overlooking the river, a great location for it. This site was always clean and very well managed by the conservation crew that worked there. It never looked like an over-camped site, and we always left it cleaner than when we got it.

1985. My two friends and me. Otter Brook is behind us,
and the fireplace is to the lower left, overlooking the river.

This campsite on Otter Brook is another favorite spot for listening to the natural music of Otter Brook and smelling the campfire from a hammock. True R&R

1985 photo of Otter Brook bridge. It was 14 years old.

I took my friends on a few hikes to Squaw Lake and Icehouse Pond, both of which are beautiful locations that I highly recommend. Icehouse Pond is a short hike. Squaw Lake was originally a 0.45-mile hike from its trailhead in 1985. However, this changed in 2010, when a new trailhead was established, extending the hike to approximately 1.5 miles. Due to the washout of the Falls Pond outlet, it is now a good 3+ mile hike.

Squaw Lake offers excellent fishing opportunities if you can find the fishing spots. While the sandy shore may appear inviting for swimming, don't! There are leeches, which can sometimes be seen in the shallow waters near the shore. The site itself is stunning and ideal for an overnight stay. we were entertained by the loons on the lake in their natural habitat

Photo of Squaw Lake. There's always a loon or two on this lake.

Back at our site #118, We had a bear moseying around our camp just at dark. We heard rocks moving in the river while we were sitting by the fire. Then, five minutes later, he was 20 feet behind us in the woods. My friend asked, "Is he going to eat us?"

I laughed and said, "He is just being curious, but no."

Luckily, black bears are mostly omnivorous. They eat plants: Berries, fruit, nuts, acorns, leaves, roots, sedges, grasses, and plant tubers. They also eat human food, garbage and pet food, as well as small animals like insects, fish, frogs, reptiles, small mammals, birds, and bird eggs. But they can smell food from over a mile away.

The most important thing is to leave them alone; just observe them, as they are more afraid of you than you are of them. DO NOT TRY TO FEED THEM or throw your food scraps into the woods by your campsite. You or the next family/group camping might have an unexpected guest.

1985. Getting fresh water from the spring. Old milk can, uphill gravity-style, installed back in the mid '60s or early '70s. It's still there today,and although it hasn't been tested for drinking in years it's good for washing at your campsite. There were four black pipe springs within the MRP. Now only two are left.

Natural fed mountain spring water

I remember that in 1985, the Cellar Mountain area was acquired by the state from International Paper. The trail to Cellar Pond runs through this area. Prior to the sale, International Paper harvested 80% of the forest on the hill along the road leading up to the log road, which is now the trail-head.

I am not for clear cutting in a forest, but I do support a well-managed harvesting that makes the forest a healthy, flourishing one.

In 1986, I was on a fall hunting trip with my dad and crew. We set up our camp at site #73, right off the loop road to Bear Pond Trail. I took along a good friend, Steve, for his first time into the Moose River Plains. He had never been exposed to the wilderness and wildlife, and he was amazed at the remoteness of the area. Bear Pond Trail wasn't a marked or main-tained trail at that time, as it was still private land, but there was a barrier at the wet, swampy entry. We walked the old loop trail that brings you over to the Red River sand pit below campsite #77. After that trip, we went camping every Memorial Day opening for 10 days for the next five years in a row, recreating. I'd always invite people from the city to come on a trip with me to give them a chance to get away from the city grind and be in a place to unwind in the outdoors, camping.

1986. Hunting, late fall, campsite #77.
From left to right Me, Kevin, Steve, Artie, Hank and Sr Joe

70   Adirondack Memoir

1988-1990

I always invited and encouraged people to take a trip with me to expose them to the wilderness and the great outdoors. My friend Louie decided to come up with me and my friend Steve.

Again, Louie was someone who had never been away from city life on a wilderness camping trip. I warned him about the blackflies, and gave him a quick crash course about smart camping and the wildlife that we could encounter.

One thing I told them was, "Do not soak yourself in your sweet cologne, you'll be eaten alive by blackflies!" Well, that night in the tent all we heard was Louie scratching all night. He literally was "bugging out." "I told you they would eat you alive," I said. The next day I made him take a swim in the South Branch of the Moose River. The cold water would help relieve the itching.

Here's a little information based on personal experiences with black flies:
- In early spring, do your walks in the early morning and later afternoon/evening.
- Wear light colored clothes (white and gray).
- Pull your socks over your pants
- Don't wear cologne
- Keep a smoky fire going!
- FACT: only the female black flies bite. They require a blood meal to develop their eggs. The male black flies do not bite, and instead feed on nectar from plants.
- Blackflies are a bit claustrophobic, so wear a brimmed hat or screening over your face. Old Woodsman and OFF! Deep Woods both help.

The new concrete bridge had just been finished after the culverts were washed out two years earlier, in 1988, after a rapid early spring/late winter snow melt.

After Louie's swim, I took them on an old logging road bushwhack hike down Benedict Brook to see a few old large pine trees that had never been logged. The old logging road starts behind site #67. There was an old logging camp there, past it about a mile or so to an open section of Benedict.

With my friend "Terry" with one of the large eastern white pines over by Benedict Brook.

1990, The Main Corridor

This is how the Main Corridor looked after over 25 years of State personnel working on improving the roads, raking the entire system weekly.

All the fill needed was used from borrow sand pits. All the natural resources came from within the MRP. To me, this was a great idea rather than what happened in around 2010, when this area was reclassified to a Wild Forest. Since then, the State has been carting in foreign material (gravel) from over 50 miles away that could bring in invasive seeds that can cause significant harm to the environment, spreading and out-competing native plants and often destroying the natural balance of the habitat.

A plant that is not naturally found in a region, but can establish and cause negative impacts once it's introduced is considered invasive.

My personal thought is that natural soil should be used from within the area to maintain the roads and trails. To me, that's true conserving. "Conservation" refers to the practice of protecting and preserving natural environments and resources, essentially keeping them in their original state.

Chapter Five

Camping With Family and Friends
MRP Recreation Area
1990-2010

1990 Helldiver campsite #61, with my dad and my best friend Chris, aka "Woody."

My dad and I set up camp with my close friend Chris for a five-day stay. It was his first time in the Moose River Plains, and since he was an outdoorsman, I knew he'd love this area. At that time, the Indian Lake road was still accessible to Little Indian Lake, and we hiked the old Indian River road a few miles to the end, visiting all the old riverside campsites. It's a beautiful area, and I've observed how much the forest has grown in. (*I videoed this area on Hi8 every five years to document the rate of grow-in.*)

1990, Helldiver site #61

Then we hiked back to Little Indian lakefront campsite, where we had lunch.

Helldiver Campsite #61 is now the parking area, but it was then a campsite, the site was moved into the woods.

This was a great campsite. I camped here for a few years in a row. Not many people would drive down at the time and visit the pond, one of the most beautiful ponds in the Moose River Plains, and only a short hike. The only fish that are in this pond are small bullheads. The pond is shallow, ten feet at its deepest point, and warm, with a murky bed base. I wouldn't recommend swimming, but there's plenty of wildlife—beaver, bear, deer, and for a few years, bull moose. If you walk around this campsite a bit into the woods, there are some nice-sized eastern white pines. This campsite was always quiet. The campsite coyotes would be out every night. The trail to the pond was wet and boggy as you got closer to the pond, but in 2010 it was completely done over with gravel, and a dock was installed. The trail is handicap accessible.

1990, Helldiver site #61

Helldiver Pond is all bullheads.

Doing some target practice at the sand pit with my Dad and Chris, aka "Woody."

The South Branch Moose River bridge was replaced
in 1990 after a washout in 1988-1989.

The South Branch Moose River bridge was replaced
in 1990 after a washout in 1988-1989.

Campsite #76A in the Red Plains area, 1990. It was an old road that went along the balsam-pine mixed forest edge and ran parallel to a log road to what is now the Mitchell Pond Loop. It's much overgrown with thick brush now.site is very small, off the main road, with a beautiful view and was closed in the mid '70s by Forest Ranger Gary Lee (now retired)to protect a Golden Eagle that was nesting in the area for a few years and it's still closed.

78   Adirondack Memoir

2000-2003 photo at Helldiver Pond before the dock was installed. My daughter is fishing. This is a great place for little kids to learn how to fish. There is nothing but little bullhead fish, but they'll catch a lot of them here.2008 we met a gentleman "Terry" whom we became close friends with and have had many camping trips and good memories in the Moose River Plains.

2009. Tracking: fresh moose tracks leading to the swamp.

2008. "Giddy up, Daddy!" Helldiver Trail.

Canoeing with my daughter Lexie at Lost Ponds.

2009, My daughter Lexie at Otter Brook. Recreating and determined.

In 2009, I was camping at Helldiver with my daughter. We would get up early to watch the fog lift and the sun rise on the pond. My daughter spotted a big bull moose across the pond. We slowly paddled our canoe in its direction to get a little closer but stayed a safe distance. We were as quiet as we could be so as not to disturb him, but just watch, observe, and video him feeding and swimming around the pond's edge. We watched him for about an hour. We kept his location private so he wouldn't get spooked from his home and become a tourist attraction, and we only told three NYDEC conservation officers, who later that day came to our campsite to see the videos we took, which we uploaded on YouTube a few weeks later with the title "Moose in Pond" and an undisclosed location. This was to protect his territory from being disturbed by tourists.

The following year, 2010, we went to two of the public hearings on the reclassification about to be made to the Moose River Plains, changing it from a Recreational Area to a Wild Forest area, with all the added restrictions under that classification. At one of the meetings, my daughter mentioned that we had seen a big bull moose in an undisclosed location somewhere in the Moose River Plains.

Sadly, about a year later, the word got out and he was in the news. He became a tourist attraction and high-resolution video and music uploads on YouTube attracted 25-30 people at the pond on a daily basis, all looking for him. The news even gave him a name—SMH—we haven't camped at that location since.

Helldiver Pond is in a beautiful setting, and is full of wildlife. I saw beaver, bear, deer, coyote, Great Blue Heron and moose. We have seen many moose in all different areas within the Moose River Plains.

Here are a few facts about moose: They move around mostly at dawn and at dusk. I've noticed that the time I've seen them most is when it cools down, with a big temperature drop from a warm day, and when there's a heavy dew/fog. Bulls will move more during their rut season, which is mid to late fall. They will be often seen in wetlands feeding on plants and pond lilies, and will eat Balsam Fir in the winter, when they tend to stay in the pines, which provides good shelter during the winter months.

These photos are from 2009 and show the Bull Moose my daughter Lexie discovered. We observed him at 5am. The light conditions were poor and the photos were taken with a box camera

08/05/2009

08/05/2009

This photo of moose tracks on the road was taken around 6AM.
Once this road is graveled, you won't be seeing
any more wildlife tracks.

Chapter Six

MRP Reclassified as a Wild Forest and

More Road and Campsite Closures

VSA

2010-2024

In 2010, more changes were made in the Moose River Plains, again closing more road access to primitive areas and many campsites in desired locations, as it was reclassified from a Recreation Area to a "Wild Forest." To conform to the "Master Plan "and its regulations, a few miles of access roads were closed from just below Squaw Lake to the end of Little Indian Lake, limiting access to Squaw Lake, Muskrat Pond and Little Indian Lake and about ten campsites. These changes also made the hike to the Indian River area and Balsam, Stink and Horn lakes inaccessible unless you are perfectly fit for that kind of adventure down an unmanaged and unmarked trail.

My family and I attended both public hearings in Inlet and Indian Lake regarding this change voicing our disagreement with it and our opinion that it should be left as it was and aligned with its 1963 original intentions, that is, as a managed forest in a "Recreation Area." All access to its remote areas was never supposed to be closed, like roads and campsite closures that were done in the past in 1980, restricting hunters, fishermen, outdoor enthusiasts, the elderly, handicapped, disabled veterans and future generations from being able to access this remote primitive area.

Every ten years, public access is being reduced in the Moose River Plains for those who are unable to walk the many miles now required to be in this deep, remote primitive area. The Moose River Plains is a very unique place and should be treated as such. Campsites on water and far distances apart and off the main road are the most desirable for outdoor wilderness enthusiasts who want a true nature experience.

Mitchell and Helldiver ponds both had trail work for handicap access, and new docks. My personal recommendation was that the Helldiver dock should have had flotation under it and not piers as footers to the pond's bed, which is a muddy bog bed and will keep sinking.

2010

I visited with Shawn Hansen, Inlet Highway Department Supervisor and his work crew, including Kyle O'Connor and other staff employees, who now do pre-season campsite cleaning and have taken over managing and maintaining all of the main roads from Inlet all the way up to the Silver Run campsite #23-#24 area, where the Indian Lake and the Hamilton County highway departments take over and manage the area to the Cedar River Flow and the road over Otter Brook (Indian Lake Road).

After 2000, I did start to notice the roads getting a bit rough, and vegetation over-growing on the shoulders, as the state didn't do as much maintenance and management as they did in the early years, the mid '60s through the 1990s.

The next photo was taken in 2011 at the Falls Pond outlet, where the Hamilton County Highway Department had just replaced a culvert pipe that washed out in a fall rainstorm. It washed out again in 2020. It's downstream, about 300 feet in the woods, and still has not been fixed, but I'm told it's still on the State's list to be replaced with an engineered bridge.

2011. Falls Pond outlet. Just finished a new culvert again. It needs a good bridge.

2010, Walking Otter Brook road with family

2010. Brandon following his dad's footsteps walking Otter Brook Road and Truck Trail, whistling the Andy Griffith Show theme song.

2010. Rock walking downstream at Otter Brook with Brandon, aka my "boi."

The trail to Icehouse Pond was recently redone, as well as the campsite on the pond. It's a short, easy trail and is accessible for anyone in a wheelchair. The old deer exclosure from the 1970s is still there. Back in the late 1960s, the State reduced the herd size and set up a deer enclosure. This pond is a great place to fish for trout. I used to hunt this area when the grass meadow was much lower. (*The deer exclosure off the trail was used for forest habitat management.*)

2010. Fall foliage. Hiked the newly redone trail to
Icehouse Pond and checked out the new campsite.

2010, Hiking to Helldiver Pond with the family.

2010, Helldiver Pond

2010, Beaver Hut. Helldiver Pond is teeming with wildlife, including bear, deer, beaver, Great Blue Heron, and moose. It's a short, rewarding hike that is also handicap accessible.

2010, My kids Lexie and Brandon singing, dancing and playing in the rain.

My daughter Lexie loved playing in the mud, making what she called a "Witches' Brew," using sticks, leaves, pine needles and pine cones. I loved just letting my kids be kids, living it up and making great family memories!

In 2010, my daughter Lexie wanted to take a day hike into the West Canada Wilderness Area, so I took her on a hike to Falls Pond. I hadn't been there in over 20 years. It's accessible from the trailhead as you cross Otter Brook Bridge. In a mile or so you'll come to the trailhead just on the side of the road, about 500 feet from the Falls Pond Outlet. The first part of the trail runs parallel to Falls Pond Outlet, with very nice scenery. Most of the trail is in a hardwood setting.

2010, Trail-head to Falls Pond

After about 1.5 miles on the trail, the last half mile there requires some bushwhacking until you get to the pond, which is in a beautiful pine bed setting.

Beaver pond along the way to Falls Pond. The best way to get a good hiking stick is to find one cut by a beaver from their dam.

On the trail. You can see the old remains of bulkhead logs that supported a log bridge many years ago. There are just two walking boards installed on it now.

Just as you approach Falls Pond, a nice pine bed pond/lakeside site.

Lexie in the sun, eyes closed, both arms up,
taking deep breaths of that clean, fresh Adirondack air.

Falls Pond

Falls Pond

Falls Pond

In 2011, I took my daughter Lexie on a hike to Squaw Lake. At that time it was reasonably accessible, only about a half-mile hike from the parking area on Little Indian Lake Road, where we camped for the day. We had a nice campfire cookout and observed a loon all day, singing and swimming. I told my daughter, "We just observe them and don't disturb them. This is their home and we are their guests." It's a beautiful lake and a "must" place to visit and hike to. It's a great trail for families with kids, and it has a beautiful lakeside campsite. There is a nice sandy clearwater shore, but as I mentioned earlier, don't be fooled. There are leeches in that lake. I do not recommend going for a swim! The road has been closed since 2011. It's now about three miles from Falls Pond Outlet.

Squaw Lake trailhead

The Squaw Lake trail is mostly downhill from the road, with a mix of terrain rocks, wetland, and pine bed. The campsite at Squaw Lake is well worth the hike. I highly recommend it. It's a gorgeous site.

Squaw Lake campsite

Photo of the old boat, still on the shore at Squaw Lake.
This is a stunning lake, where you can listen to the loons calling and wailing.

2012. Helldiver Pond dock is two years old. Lexie and Brandon are enjoying it at sunset.

2012. Hiking with my kids to spend the day and do some canoeing,
fishing and lunch at Lost Ponds. I notice that trails are not being managed and kept cut back.
They're slowly growing in, making it tough for any fire or search and rescue access.

Someone's getting a free ride to Lost Ponds.

Lexie at Lost Ponds. Another beautiful pond, a short easy hike, and well worth it. The fishing is great once you find the fishing hole. There is also an amazing echo. HELL-OOOO!

2012. Passing on our traditional Adirondack Homefries recipe to the next generation. Good quality family time.

2013, The Beal Family at Otter Brook

Joanne and I inspecting the outhouses.

2015. Lost Ponds. I taught my son Brandon how to build a lookout fort. He built it using some dead pine lying in the woods and some rope.

Teaching my son firearms and safety at the sand pit.

"Hey Dad, what is it called when I shoot it right in the middle?" "Bullseye!"

Good grouping.

Eastern (red-spotted) newt.

2015. Walked the grassy banks about 1.5 miles down Sumner Stream, doing some fishing.

Here's a time capsule of my kids on the Lost Ponds trail.
I have good memories of watching them grow up.

2015. Log bridge built over the old log bridge in 1977 on the trail to Lost Ponds.

Beaver Lake

2015. With my Boi on a hike to Beaver Lake. This is another great trail, good for families with kids. Walk through a mature mix of yellow birch and pine. This old pine is right on the trail.

2013. The same tree. Lexie, Brandon (aka "Boi") and Noah, our pup.

Photo looking over South Branch Moose River on the trail to Beaver Lake.

There are the remains of an old stone well house as you approach the lake. Further down the hill, there is an open field where the Wilcox camp once stood. To the left is the campsite by the lake.

Photo looking over South Branch Moose River on the trail to Beaver Lake.

Hiking along the Otter Brook bank for a mile or so. Lexie and Noah.

Lexie and Noah, Otter Brook

The next photo was taken in 2016 at the South Branch Moose River campsite #87, one of the most popular campsites being on water, of which there are very few of these in a primitive wilderness area. I'm not a big water campsite camper, but I have camped on them I can understand the beauty and attraction of these sites. Over the years, this site has slowly been washing away due to nature's rage of the river during heavy rainstorms and the site's location on a bend. *In my personal opinion, there should be more waterfront sites, since they are the most desirable. People should write letters requesting more sites. Let your voice be heard.*

Campsite #87, South Branch Moose River

2016. Camp set up at Lost Ponds.

Tonight's menu: Brook trout caught by Brandon on Sumner Stream.

2016. Picking sweet wild blueberries, mid-July. There's nothing better tasting than fresh-picked, sweet wild blueberries. Mid-July is the perfect time to pick them.

Wild blueberries are small, about the size of a pea, but really juicy and sweet.

2016. We used the wild blueberries we'd picked to make blueberry pancakes.

2016. Stargazing and watching shooting stars by the campfire while we told stories.

How to make your campfire colorful.

2016. Brandon betting on the snail race.

Drive in to sites #53-#55. There's some history still around this site, an old slab from the tractor and truck repair building and old sleigh rails off in the woods from the 1940s.

Since 2000, we've lived closer to the places I love. The Moose River Plains is a few minutes away. Now we camp a few times every summer, all around the Plains.

Site #53. A newer fireplace, only two years old. It is not as heavy-duty as they were in the '70s, but is more useful and more desirable than fire rings, and the fire is more contained.

Joanne and Lexie staying toasty on a chilly late August morning.

2016, Rock Dam. My daughter Lexie: "I can't get wet."

Family tradition—Lexie learning how to drive in the Moose River Plains.

Hiking on the Indian River Road/Trail with my kids.

I've got my dinner!

Noah got his fish, too!

2016. Hiking to Bear Pond.

2017
SOMEONE LEFT A CAMPSITE & THE FIRE WAS STILL BLAZING SO WE STAYED UNTIL IT WAS OUT
MOOSE RIVER PLAINS

2017. Someone packed up their campsite and left with the campfire in a blaze, so we stayed with it until it had burned down and then we used our water jug to completely extinguish it. Please make sure your fire is completely extinguished when you leave.

2017. Tree fungus memory, camp art.

2017. Another Eastern (red-spotted) Newt.
We hiked six miles down to the Indian River Road, and along the way Brandon
counted 257 newts and spotted a bald eagle and some moose tracks

2017. Day hike to Whites Pond

2017. Hiking Otter Brook rock banks with my "Boi.

2017. We had a night adventure walking the road and listening to a bobcat do its screech/yell, coyotes in the distance, and looking for a big American Toad.

2017. Walking off the beaten path at sunset on an old log road, looking at Mitchell Mountain.

Some Fun Facts for Kids

What's the difference between frogs and toads?

While frogs and toads are both amphibians, all toads are frogs, but not all frogs are toads.

How can you tell the difference?

One of the biggest physical differences between frogs and toads is their skin. While frogs have smooth or slimy skin that is moist, toads have thicker, bumpy skin that is usually dry. The differences in their skin are because of their typical environments. Frogs spend more time in the water, or are usually very close to water while on land, so their skin stays moist. Toads, on the other hand, spend more time on land and travel further from water.

A big difference between frogs and toads is that all toads are poisonous, while frogs are not. Toads have parotid glands behind their eyes that secrete toxins. These toxins permeate their skin, so you can come into contact with them if you pick them up,

Most of the toxins are mild to humans, but you should always wash your hands thoroughly with soap and water after handling a toad.

2017. Fall foliage. Walking Sumner Stream.

Canoeing down Sumner Stream.

2018. Sumner Stream.

2018. Canoeing down Benedict Brook with my "Boi."
Be prepared to do some portaging for a bit a few miles down it opens up
with beautiful large pines.I hope it had a permit to cut those live trees!

2018. Site on Lost Pond. I put a coat of protectant on this lakefront picnic table every year to help keep it preserved for everyone to use.

2018. Bushwhacking an old log road with more old history left behind.

2018. Bushwhacking an old log road with more old history left behind.

2018. Walking the banks down Bradley Brook,
a beautiful area with a brook running through a pine forest.

2018. A young cow moose. My son and I watched her taking her time wandering down the road.

2018. Fresh signs of a busy beaver. Trees are a main source of their diet as well as some vegetation. I hope it had a permit to cut those live trees!

2019. I took my son on a hike to Muskrat Pond. The metal sign behind him used to be wooden, but bears chewed the wooden signs, so they were all replaced with metal ones.

Muskrat Pond

Muskrat Pond

At the sand/borrow pit target practice. Back in the 1970s-late '80s, this was where you would go for target practice.

2019. Site #87. Nature is slowly washing it away.

2019. A fire ring was installed, but it didn't last long. It was gone the following year. Concrete stone fireplaces are my personal preference for an area like the MRP.

2020 camping. Ready for the day's adventure.

2020. Just finished setting up the campsite. Brandon and Amber, our pup.

Met our friend Terry. Hiked to Lost Ponds and went bushwacking on a few old log roads off the main trail.

2020. Sumner Stream. Very low water table. You could walk the river's banks.

Walking the river banks at Sumner Stream.

2020. Walking around the old sandpit tracking moose and coyote.

2020. At the Falls Pond Outlet culvert washout, Indian Lake Road.

2020. At the Falls Pond Outlet culvert washout, Indian Lake Road.

Falls Pond Outlet. The culvert pipe is downstream about 300 feet in the woods. It's still there.

Falls Pond Outlet

Falls Pond Outlet

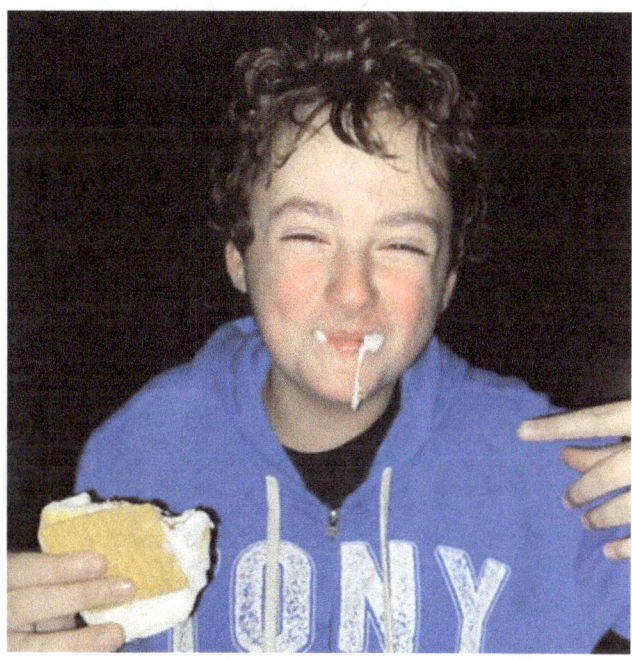
When you're camping, your trip isn't complete until you have your S'mores.

A 1940 Dodge resting down an old logging road off the main road near campsite site #37. There's another old road that runs through site #39, Kenwell's Loop Trail. Where there was once a camp, now there's a clearing.

1940 Dodge off an old Logging Road.

Geographical elevation plate which is just off the side of the road. Everyone drives right by it. I think the first time I saw it was 1971-72. It was broken back then as well. That's why sometimes by walking the road a bit, you get better details of what's in your surroundings.

The official Bigfoot Response Team walking the road. You never know!

Gould Paper Company used old kerosene tankers as culvert pipes throughout this area.
They would cut the ends off and use them as a culvert.
This one has been at Benedict Creek since the 1950s.

2021. Hiking an old log road I did as a kid now with my Boi
exploring the history left behind of an old logging camp.

Some of the history at Kenwell's Camp.

More history at Kenwell's Camp.

1944. Kenwell's Camp.

2021. Kenwell's Camp location. We met a gentleman who always wanted to see
Kenwell's camp but never could find it so we told him to come and follow us.

In 2021, I was camping again with longtime friend Chris at Lost Ponds. In 1988, it was the first time I took him on a camping trip to the Moose River Plains, he said, "If it takes more than two hours to get there, I'm not going." So I said, "You're in luck, it's only two hours away." Driving from Long Island, we arrived five hours later. It didn't take him long to get over it. He said, "WOW!! It was well worth the drive."

2021. Chris cooking up breakfast before our hike to see some record-size pines and some wildlife observation down off Benedict Brook.

2021. The Three Stooges: Brandon, Matt and Chris at Helldiver Pond.

With my friend Chris and Brandon, walking an old log road near Bradley Brook.
There's not much left of it.

2021. A temporary footbridge was installed until an engineered bridge
could be put in for vehicles to drive to the Squaw Lake trailhead.

Helldiver Pond

The dock is settling a little more as the piers are sinking. You can't put piers on a bog base, but it's a beautiful pond, as always.

Helldiver Pond

2021. The Three Stooges: Brandon, Matt and Chris at Helldiver Pond.

2022. More tree fungus art. Camping memories.

In 2023, Squaw Lake's name was officially changed to Muskrat Lake. The term "squaw" was considered derogatory towards indigenous women, and this led to widespread efforts to remove it from geographical names across the United States. I always referred to Squaw Lake as a beautiful lake and thought it was perfect as a part of our respective Native American heritage.

Aerial view of Muskrat Lake, aka Squaw Lake.

2024

This is the most current map of the Moose River Plains Wild Forest, showing all its boundaries, campsites, roads, trails, ponds, lakes and rivers. All of the old logging/wagon roads are not shown, as they have completely grown in over the years—although my memory of their locations is still sharp. A copy of this map and all its information can be obtained at the Inlet gate registration box or at the Inlet town information center.

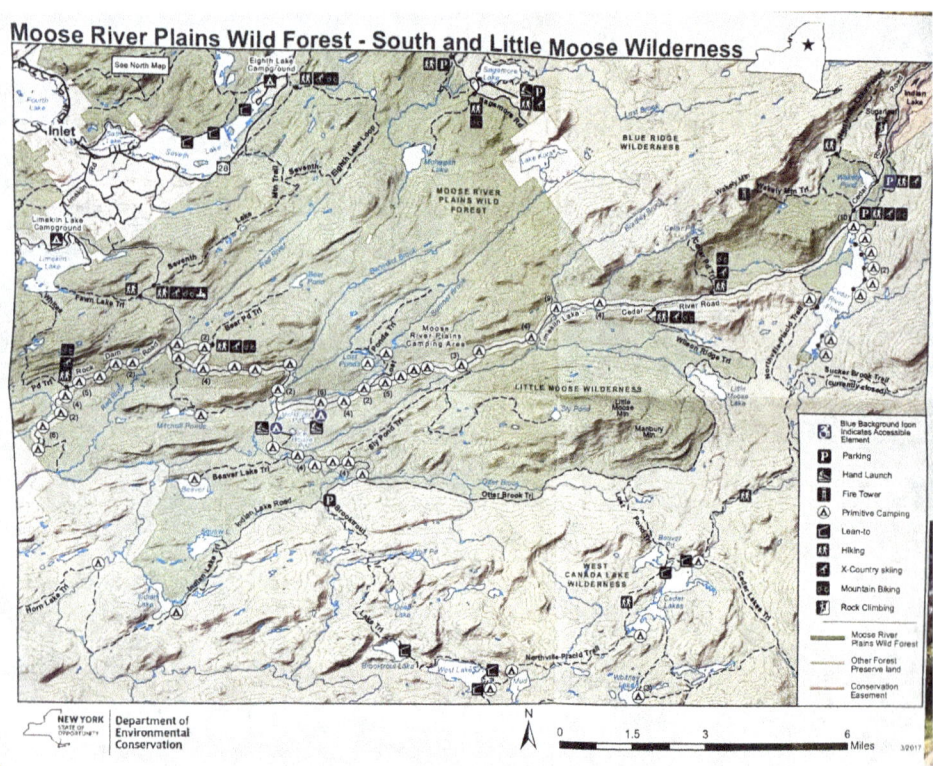

2024. My son Brandon checking out an old skidder near Silver Run.

Skidder by Silver Run behind site #22.

Here are a few pictures taken off an old logging road by Benedict Creek in 2024. There is an old Ford and some other remains. If you're looking for big, old pine trees, the area to find them is about three quarters of a mile down this old road, some bushwacking for a ½ mile.

Terry hugging that big old Eastern White Pine.

The photos on the next few pages of a more cars over by the old log road off Bradley Brook campsites #14-#18.

Camping at Silver Run, site #24.

Walking Bradley Brook banks.

My son and I did some exploring around an old, abandoned campsite #5.
It was always a wet site and rarely used because of it.

2024. Camping with my kids at Lost Ponds.

Doing some road cruising with Lexie, Brandon,
and our old-timer, 16-year-old pup Noah.

2024. Off the beaten trail through the pine forest to get
to the big old pines that were never harvested with Terry.

In 2020-2024, as a VSA in early April, I was helping Shawn Hansen, Inlet's Highway Superintendent, assess the road conditions before the gates opened for the summer season. We took a lunch break and went on a short walk on an old overgrown log road near Bradley Brook, which is no longer recognizable. As we were walking, Hansen asked "How do you know where you're going?" I replied, "You see that big rock ledge?" Hansen replied, "Yeah," I then directed him to "walk past that and in about twenty feet, look to your left." At that point, Hansen saw that there's an old car in the woods.

Shawn Hansen (Inlet's Highway Superintendent) is taking a picture, amazed at this piece of history with a story to tell.

Pre-season road work, getting roads ready for the spring/summer season.

Pre-season, unplugging a culvert pipe at the road into Lost Ponds trailhead entry.

Here, I am helping get all the roads in shape with my York Rake and side-by-side. I did all of the off-roads to drive-in campsites and trailheads, helping to keep them maintained and make the area a better place for everyone!

2024, early May. Raking Icehouse Pond trailhead.

2024. Filling in some holes and raking the road in to campsites #53-#55. It hadn't been raked or maintained in over 35- 40 years.

2024, Moose River, South Branch. Doing VSA work on all the bridge guardrails and assessing their condition in the Moose River Plains.

2024, Red River. Cleaning up vegetation and painting the guardrails.

As a VSA, I make observations and recommendations to NYSDEC about what needs attention. One suggestion was to address the Otter Brook Bridge. Some maintenance is needed to preserve the future structural integrity and to remove some of the algae/moss. Once established, mosses hold moisture that deteriorates the concrete surface beneath and shortens the lifespan of the concrete on bridges meant for long-term use.

Overgrown saplings growing on the retaining walls are also a problem, as their roots will start to push against them and start to crack the retaining walls, weakening them and affecting the bulkheads, causing failure. It's just like an old sidewalk that has been underneath trees for years. The roots eventually make it buckle.

Otter Brook Bridge retaining wall.

Site #80

2024. Campsite #80, on the old Kenwell Chapin's crossing trail that leads to the South Branch Moose River,

I added this outhouse to my list of things that needed to be reset. These minor fixes would be a great project for a Boy Scout Troop, and they could plan a great camping trip at the same time. What a great place to expose the younger generation to the beauty of the wilderness.

This campsite has some history to it, as it was one of Kenwell's old trails. There's still an old deer exclosure on the right, then Kenwell's old well remains. If you keep walking the trail, which is well-overgrown, it will take you to the South Branch Moose River. Former ranger Gary Lee cut the trail for portage access, and for years there was a small canoe carry trail sign at the campsite. It's long gone now. I walked it with my son, but it would be difficult to carry a canoe through now. I will recommend to the forester that it be recut and maintained for future access.

Over the past 20-33 years I've watched the forest grow with no forest management. I guess the plan is to just "let it grow." with very little or no forest management.

"When a forest is undermanaged and over-choked, it experiences a decline in biodiversity, increased susceptibility to disease and pests, reduced tree growth, potential for more severe wildfires, and a disruption in the natural balance of the ecosystem, often leading to a shift in species composition towards less desirable plants due to excessive competition for sunlight and nutrients."

2024. September sunset at Sumner Stream.

2024. I met up with retired ranger Gary Lee, who was the ranger in the Moose River Plains for over 35 years. Here we're going over some of the details in my book.

Gary Lee is still doing what he loves, managing wildlife.
I assisted him when he was banding Saw-Whet Owls.

164   Adirondack Memoir

Chapter Seven

Indian River Road Area, Past and Present, And My Personal Thoughts

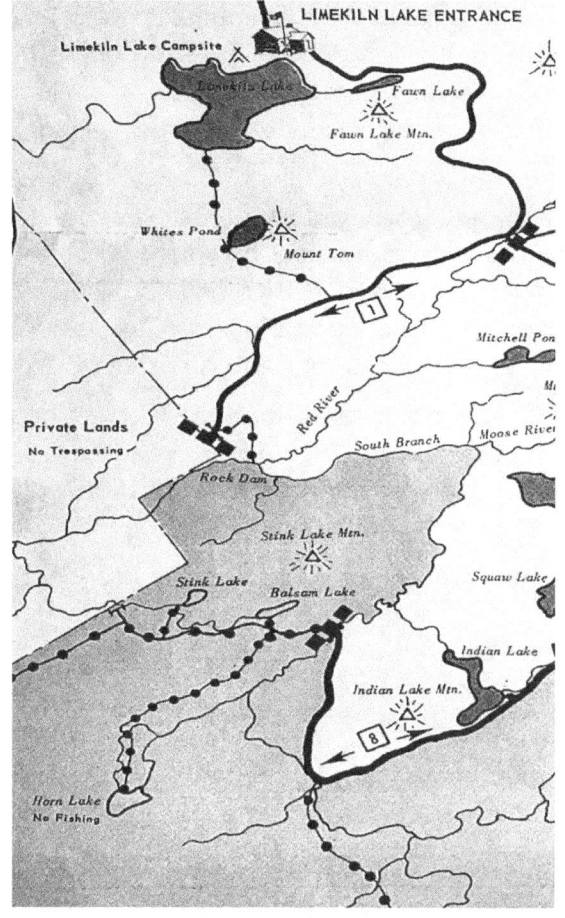

This map shows the Indian River Road, which was a primary road, and the land that started from the southwest end of Little Indian Lake, also known as Camping Area 8, primitive camping at the time. It continued to the Indian Mountain area, and went to the end barrier (three black squares), where there was access to the West Canada Wilderness Area.

The dotted lines were old log/wagon roads, all of which I walked. This area was very remote and the deepest within the Moose River Plains, with primitive campsites, plenty of wildlife, great fishing in the Indian River and a good entry point to the West Canada Wilderness Area.

Balsam, Stink, and Horn lakes and Ice Cave Mountain wagon trail were reasonably accessible for all, great for families with kids. The trail was mostly flat, with a beautiful walk through the balsam forest and with Stink Mountain in view. The lakes were gorgeous. Each one had something different to offer. Just as Helldiver is beautiful, it was also a popular area with big game hunters. It was a truly big loss for people when access was closed and the Indian River was reclassified as a wild river, and the Moose River Plains borders were absorbed into the West Canada Wilderness Area.

Now it's a forgotten part of nature's beauty that was once available for all to see. Remember, only your voices can make it possible to change it back to its original access. Let your voice be heard, so that you and the next generation can enjoy this wonderful area. As it is now, it's just about been erased as another beautiful place to go.

What follows are some photos taken from the road looking up to the first campsite, on the Indian River off Indian River Road. It was an old logging road, and a walk-in site across the footbridge overlooked the river on a ridge.

These sites were never given numbers, but if you continued from #149 it would have been #151. On the map above, where the "8" with the two arrows is, it was just below the left arrow. The dotted line was the log road that went through the campsite.

As you start heading South West from the end of little Indian Lake on your left is a old unnamed beaver pond then as the road heads north where it meets the Indian River the first campsite was on your left about 100 ft walk up to site #151

1972. Photo of Site #151. It was on the Indian River.

1973. Site #151. Picnic table is in the upper right corner on the bank.

Site #151, taken from the picnic table and looking toward the road.
It overlooked the Indian River, a truly beautiful spot.

2015. Site #151 with my daughter standing where the picnic table once was.

168   Adirondack Memoir

2021. Site #151. There was a footbridge to walk up to the campsite on the Indian River. A sandy shore is way ahead on the right. A truly beautiful spot.

2021. The Indian River.

1990. Campsite #152 on the Indian River, off Indian River Road, ten years after its closure.

Campsite #152

This photo was taken from the original drive into the campsite,
but the drive has completely grown in.

2021, Site #152, 41 years after its closure, I hike way back here every few years. It's never visited by anyone but me and my kids. This was the last campsite at the time in the Moose River Plains Indian River Road end.

2015. The fireplace at the last campsite at the end of the Indian River Road/trail.

1971. My dad Artie and our family friend Claude sitting on the last log from the log bridge as you crossed the Indian River into the Indian River Road into the West Canada Wilderness to Balsam, Stink and Horn lakes.

Along this old road was a small marsh bog pond that had floating logs going across it in the summer, but in the winter when it froze in the winter, it was used as a log truck road.

1940's.photo

Beaver meadow/pond off Indian River Road/trail.

Fall, 1980. Indian River Road, about 3.5 miles from the southwest end of Little Indian Lake, the last time it was open and accessible.

My Personal Thoughts

I've spent over fifty years observing this area's transformation. Looking ahead, I anticipate that desirable campsites will eventually close and more roads—valued by outdoor enthusiasts for access to private spots and waterfront sites—will also be shut down.

This area should have been grandfathered in and exempted from the new regulations being implemented.

The MRP could have served as a model for other wild forest areas by preserving primitive camping and maintaining its natural character, in alignment with its original purpose, thereby remaining a truly distinctive location.

There was a lot more wildlife and forest management and maintenance when the State had adequate full-time crews to care for it. Now it's under-managed. There are very minimal work crews, and now volunteers (VSAs) like me who truly love this area try to help in any way we can.

There was a lot more access to remote wilderness areas with diverse terrains and landscapes hence the name "Plains" the views are disappearing from overgrowth and forest choke, much less green vegetation and becoming more of a continuous drive through a dense forest, in the early days late 60's thru the early 80's there seem to be more Conservation forest & wildlife management /Conservation science.

In the past, the Plains was a remote wilderness area with a variety of landscapes and wide, open views, a stunning place that was accessible to people who loved the outdoors. These days, the area has changed—forests have grown thicker, and there are fewer open spaces. It's more like driving through a dense forest. Back in the late 1960s through the early 1980s, people paid extra attention to conservation and taking care of wildlife, and it was an exciting time for nature lovers.

I fully support this type of forest management, and of a healthy, breathing forest with a healthy habitat for all wildlife.

Conservation science practices in forest management primarily focus on managing forests to maintain biodiversity, ecosystem services, and long-term forest health, often achieved through strategies like selective logging, maintaining old-growth stands, protecting riparian areas, managing invasive species and controlled fire burns, and implementing fire management plans.

The Moose River Plains is a unique place. It is not your typical over-crowded public campground. It's a great place for families and friends, for quiet relaxation and time to get out and experience all the primitive wilderness has to offer.

Good memories of exploring the true wilderness will last a lifetime, and as kids grow up into adulthood and the stress of life overwhelms them, hopefully they'll sit back, take a deep breath, close their eyes for a minute, and think about a beautiful, peaceful place with happy memories. Hopefully, they'll know they can always go there at any time and pass on their appreciation of wilderness to their children and friends, making their memories with the next generation.

Hopefully it will always be there, and people like myself will continue to try to keep it fully accessible, as it was intended. This type of experience is not for everyone, but those people who want to be in the wilderness should have access to this type of experience. Outdoor enthusiasts should not be denied reasonable access to deep, remote, primitive wilderness.

Many elderly or disabled people who love the outdoors are not capable of walking many miles to remote primitive wilderness, and now there are so many areas that are inaccessible. They too should have easy access.

I thank you all for reading my life's camping memories and my memoir of the Moose River Plains. I look forward to meeting people and to you sharing with me all your camping memories.

Look for my next book, *Adirondack Hiking and Camping Guide in The Moose River Plains*, coming soon.

Matthew T. Beal